Study Guide to
The Catcher in the Rye
by J. D. Salinger

by Ray Moore

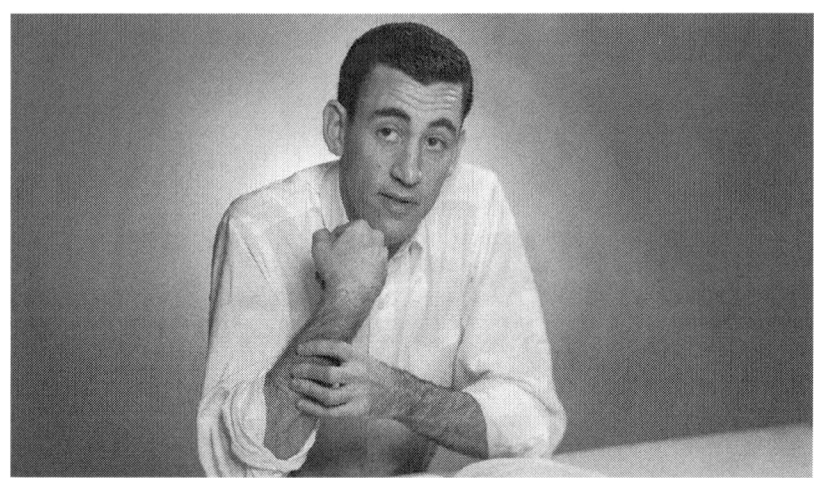

Cover photograph: J. D. Salinger in 1952, a year after *Catcher* was published, by Anthony Di Gesu (San Diego Historical Society/Hulton Archive Collection/Getty Image). This image is, to the best of my knowledge, in the public domain and is thus free for use under the Creative Commons Attribution-Share Alike 1.0 Generic license. (Source of information *The Times of Israel*.)

Copyright 2019 Ray Moore
2nd edition
All rights reserved.

Contents

Preface 1
Introduction 2
Genre 3
Dramatis Personae 4
Themes 7
Guiding Questions 9
    Chapter 1 9
    Chapter 2 11
    Chapter 3 12
    Chapter 4 12
    Chapter 5 12
    Chapter 6 13
    Chapter 7 13
    Chapter 8 13
    Chapter 9 13
    Chapter 10 13
    Chapter 11 14
    Chapter 12 14
    Chapter 13 14
    Chapter 14 14
    Chapter 15 14
    Chapter 16 15
    Chapter 17 15
    Chapter 18 16
    Chapter 19 16
    Chapter 20 16
    Chapter 21 16
    Chapter 22 16
    Chapter 23 17
    Chapter 24 17

Chapter 25	17
Chapter 26	18
General Questions	18
Reading Quizzes:	19
Chapters 1 - 4	19
Chapters 5 - 8	21
Chapters 9 - 12	22
Chapters 13 - 16	24
Chapters 17 - 20	26
Chapters 21 - 23	28
Chapters 24 - 26	29
Reading Quizzes: The Answers	31
Literary terms	35
Literary terms activity	38
Graphic organizer	41
#1 Plot	41
#2 Different perspectives	42
Revisiting A Controversial Text	43
Classroom Use of the Study Guide Questions	45
To the Reader	47

The Catcher in the Rye by J.D. Salinger

Preface

A study guide is an *aid* to the close reading of a text; it is *never* a substitute for reading the text itself. This novel deserves to be read *reflectively*, and the aim of this guide is to facilitate such a reading. The guiding questions have *no* answers provided. This is a deliberate choice. The questions are for readers who want to come to *their own conclusions* about the text and not simply to be told what to think about it by someone else. Even 'suggested' answers would limit the *exploration of the text* by readers themselves which is the primary aim of the questions.

In the classroom, I found that students frequently came up with answers that I had not even considered, and, not infrequently, that they expressed their ideas better than I could have done. The point of this guide is to *open up* the text, not to close it down by providing 'ready-made answers.' Teachers do not need their own set of predetermined answers in order effectively to evaluate the responses of their students.

The chapter notes briefly explain the most important names and references in the novel, and the introductory commentaries point to the most significant points of selected chapters. The commentaries make no claim to be complete and certainly not to be definitive. Feel free to disagree.

Acknowledgements

Brief quotations from the novel are made to support the writer's analysis. To the best of my knowledge, this constitutes 'fair use.' The text of *David Copperfield* is in the public domain. As always, I am indebted to the work of numerous reviewers and critics. Where I am conscious of having taken an idea or a phrase from a particular author, I have cited the source. Any failure to do so is an omission which I will immediately correct if it is drawn to my attention.

I believe that all quotations used fall under the definition of 'fair use.' If I am in error on any quotation, I will immediately correct it.

Thanks are due to my wife, Barbara, for reading the manuscript, for offering valuable suggestions, and for putting the text into the correct formats for publication. Any errors which remain are my own.

Spoiler alert!

If you are reading the novel for the first time, you may wish to go straight to the Guiding Questions section and refer to the other sections later since they do explain everything that happens in the novel, including the ending. Of course, you can read this guide in any order you want to.

A Note on the graphic organizers:

Two graphic organizers are provided to enable the students to make notes. Some simple guidance will be needed depending on how the teacher wants them to be used.

A Study Guide
Introduction
Plot Summary:
Set in the 1950s, sixteen-year-old Holden Caulfield returns to New York having been expelled from his fourth prep school for unsatisfactory academic progress. He avoids seeing his parents but looks up a lot of people, some of whom he knew in the past. He seems to be frantically trying to make a connection with someone - and repeatedly failing. He does manage to meet up with his ten-year-old sister, Phoebe, who finally brings him to his senses. He goes home and seeks treatment for his psychological problems.

Why Read this Book?
This is one of the great novels of the twentieth century. Not only that, it is a novel that, from the very first, has had a particular appeal for young people.
Holden Caulfield is *not* presented as a hero or as being right. The kid has received psychiatric care and goes back into a sanatorium.

Important: Issues with this Book.
When it first appeared in 1945, *The Catcher in the Rye* proved to be controversial. Those who were offended by it pointed to Holden's use of slang and profanity, the depiction of adolescent sexuality, and perhaps more fundamentally to what they saw as the author's attack on traditional cultural values (family, education, religion, etc.). Efforts to restrict access to the book, for example, by banning it from school and public libraries, continue to the present, though as often happens they have probably had the effect of making readers more anxious to get hold of it. The novel was immediately popular particularly with young people who found in Holden a symbol for their own rebellion against a society with which they found themselves increasingly at odds during the 1950s and 60s.

This is one of the most controversial books a high school teacher might want to use, although it has no graphic sex (characters just talk about it) and no graphic violence (two deaths are reported). The main objection is to the language that the 17-year-old Holden uses in his narrative and to the attitudes that he takes to adults and the establishment which can be characterized as subversive. Since those who object to the book are not likely to be persuaded, the teacher has to take a carefully thought out decision.

The Catcher in the Rye by J.D.Salinger

Genre

The Catcher in the Rye is a bildungsroman, a novel that "relates the growing up or 'coming of age' of a sensitive person who goes in search of answers to life's questions with the expectation that these will result from gaining experience of the world" (Wikipedia). What makes the novel highly original is that Holden spends most of his time resisting growing up. The reason for this, it becomes clear as the novel progresses, is that he has been traumatized and made acutely aware of the fragility of life by the death of his younger brother Allie from leukemia and by the suicide of James Castle, a school student, who was wearing one of Holden's sweaters when he jumped to his death. As a result, Holden is terrified by the idea of change and disappearance. He admits that he hates change (he loves the Museum of Natural History because everything is always in the same place), but is not aware than his rejection of the adult world and his desire to protect little children by keeping them safe in their innocent world is motivated by his fear of adulthood.

Despite his own best efforts, his encounters in the book finally lead him to the beginnings of a more mature understanding of the true nature of childhood, adolescence and adulthood.

A Study Guide

Dramatis Personae

For a relatively short novel, *The Catcher in the Rye* has an impressively long list of characters. This reflects the fact that Holden encounters a lot of people, though he appears to *know* very few of them. (Very minor characters are excluded from the list below.)

The Caulfield Family:

Mother and Father - They remain shadowy figures who are never named. From Holden's education at a succession of private prep schools, and from the way Phoebe is always well dressed, we can conclude they are rich. His father is a corporate lawyer who invests money in Broadway shows that always flop. (As with everything in the novel, we have only Holden's word for this). Holden says that his father left the Catholic Church when he married, so Holden's mother is not Catholic. Holden describes her as neurotic, tracing her condition to the death of her youngest son.

Holden - The protagonist and narrator is a 17-year-old telling his story from a sanitarium in California where he has been sent for treatment following a mental breakdown. The narrative appears to be part of his therapy.

As a 16-years-old, Holden has just been expelled from an expensive boarding school called Pencey Prep - a pattern that has repeated itself four times. Holden is a very troubled teen (and not therefore a reliable narrator) who is desperately trying to come to terms with a world he finds full of hypocrites and phonies. As a result he is, not surprisingly, socially isolated: the only people who meet his high standards are his deceased brother, Allie, and his sister, Phoebe, both of whom he idolizes. He seems to have a morbid fear of touching and of being touched by others, is rampantly homophobic, and desperately wants to have sex but cannot bring himself to because he can only have sex with someone he respects and sex does not seem a particularly respectful activity to him.

Two events in his life have had a devastating psychological effect - the death of his brother Allie from cancer, and the suicide of one of his schoolmates, James Castle, who jumped to his death wearing Holden's turtleneck sweater. However, even these traumas do not fully explain Holden's psychological state. He has previously gone through therapy and psychoanalysis without apparent improvement.

Phoebe - Holden's sister is ten. He loves her dearly and she returns his love - pretty much unconditionally. Holden desperately wants to protect Phoebe from what he sees as the cruelties of the world, but in many ways she is the more mature and well balanced of the two and does what she can to protect Holden from himself and from the wrath of his father. It is her willingness to go along with him at the end that finally brings Holden to his senses enough to realize that he needs treatment.

Allie - Holden's younger brother died of leukemia on July 18, 1946, three years before the start of the narrative. He was 13. Holden has a very deep respect and

The Catcher in the Rye by J.D. Salinger

love for Allie and is tormented by his death. Allie died as a "kid" and remains, in Holden's memory, perpetually pure and innocent, brilliant and smart.

D.B. - Holden's older brother served in World War II and came back pretty traumatized by the experience. He is currently writing for Hollywood movies, which Holden regards as the ultimate sell-out because before moving to Hollywood, he published a book of short stories that Holden admires very much. D.B. has become just another adult phony.

Characters at Elkton Hills School and Pencey Prep:

Mr. Haas – The headmaster of Elkton Hills, Holden's former school.

Mr. Antolini - Holden's English teacher at Elkton, he now teaches at New York University. Holden respects him and looks to him for guidance because he is not like the other teachers who talk down to Holden. However, when Holden visits him, certain aspects of Mr. Antolini's personal life seem questionable to him (e.g., he drinks a lot), and when he wakes up to find Mr. Antolini touching his head, Holden is convinced that his former teacher is making a sexual pass at him. It is unclear whether this is real or all in Holden's twisted mind - he says that this sort of advance happens a lot in his life, which seems unlikely.

Lillian Antolini - Mr. Antolini's wife is significantly older than is her husband, not attractive, but very rich.

James Castle - The student at Elkton who killed himself by jumping out of his window after an argument with another student.

Dr. Thurmur - The Headmaster of Pencey Prep and the ultimate "phony" (Holden's word for people he considers to be hypocritical fakes). His daughter, another phony, is called **Thelma**.

Ossenburger - The rich alumnus owns funeral parlors and gives the students boring inspirational speeches about applying oneself and praying. A phony.

Mr. Spencer - Holden's history teacher at Pencey is an old man who tries to get Holden to play by the rules and get back on track academically, but fails to understand him and ends up just lecturing Holden.

Ward Stradlater - Holden's roommate at Pencey is handsome, popular, and (unlike Holden) sexually experienced - in fact, everything that Holden is not. Holden describes him as very pushy and obsessed with "sexy stuff." The way he makes out with girls seems to be little short of rape, and Holden is definitely not pleased when Stradlater dates his old friend Jane Gallagher. So Stradlater is an unsympathetic character, but we only have Holden's word for what he is like.

Robert Ackley - The way Holden describes this boy, who lives in the room next to Holden's, makes him sound really unattractive (pimply skin, bad teeth, annoying habits), and yet, paradoxically, Holden chooses to spend a lot of time with him. For example, he invites Ackley to come to the movies with him and Mal Brossard, and after Stradlater punches Holden in the nose, Holden goes into Ackley's room because he needs someone to talk to.

Ernest Morrow – Holden calls him the "biggest bastard" at Pencey. He meets

Ernest's mother by chance on the train to New York and lies about his relationship with Ernest.

The Girls in Holden's Life:

Jane Gallagher - Holden met her one summer when their families rented neighboring summer houses in Maine. They had a summer romance, spent a lot of time together, and Holden liked her very much - which is probably why they never had sex. Holden suspects Jane's drunken step-father of abusing her, but it is never clear whether that happened. She is one of those characters whom Holden idealizes; he continually thinks about and even plans getting in touch with her, but he never does.

Sally Hayes - A very attractive girl whom Holden has known and dated for a long time. He is conflicted in his attitude to her, finding her attractive but disliking her conventional attitudes. Holden comes up with a fantasy of the two of them running away to New England and living in the woods; Sally takes the sensible view of things and refuses.

Characters in New York City:

The Two Nuns - Holden's chance encounter with the nuns brings out his better self. He talks intelligently about *Romeo and Juliet* and sympathizes with the poverty of the nuns. They are amongst the few characters in the book with whom Holden manages to make a connection, and on the face of it the two most unlikely ones. They do not fit the stereotype he has of nuns.

Faith Cavendish – A former stripper whom Holden calls to arrange a date when he gets to New York.

Bernice, Marty and Laverne - Three young women Holden meets in the Lavender Room. They really are not interested in a sixteen-year-old.

Maurice - The elevator operator at the Edmont Hotel pimps prostitutes to hotel clients. He cheats Holden out of five dollars.

Sunny - She is the young prostitute Holden hires through Maurice, in a desperate attempt to lose his virginity. Of course, Holden cannot bring himself to have sex with her because she is just a kid; to Holden she is a sad individual rather than a prostitute. She is one of a number of women in the book with whom Holden unsuccessfully attempts to connect.

Carl Luce - Holden contacts his former student advisor at the Whooton School, who is now a student at Columbia, and tries to get him to talk about sex at their meeting, which he is only too happy to do while pretending to be too sophisticated for that stuff. Holden wonders if Carl is gay, but then he wonders that about most males.

The Catcher in the Rye by J.D.Salinger
Themes
Phoniness
Young adults instinctively 'get' Holden because they sympathize with his criticism of the values of adults - all of those clichés about being a team player, working hard at school and reaping the rewards, etc., etc. The Establishment represents everything that turns Holden off about society, and much that he says is true, but his condemnation of society is so sweeping that it leaves him nowhere to go.

Alienation and Isolation
Holden responds to stressfulsituations (or at least to the situations he *perceives* as stressful) by running away – from a succession of schools ... to the city ... to the woods. He wants no part of the hypocrisy he sees around him, but he *only* sees hypocrisy around him. This is at least partly explained as a reaction to the death of Allie: Holden avoids all attachment to people so as never to be hurt again by their sudden death. The result is a loneliness that he can never escape and eventually leads to mental breakdown.

Women and Sex
Like many young men of his age, with raging hormones, Holden wants to experience sex – after all lots of his peers have had sex (or at least they *claim* to have had sex), and he feels that he is missing out on something. The trouble is that Holden associates women with purity (or at least those oarethe only kinds of women he feels attracted to) and sex with being something crummy. Thus, he could not have sex with Jane because he idealizes her, but he cannot have sex with Sunny because he cannot separate the act from the person - she is too obviously a young kid whom he cannot respect. In addition, Holden has this thing about touching people and (especially) about being touched by them, which makes sex a bit of a problem. The result is that he lives in a state of almost continual sexual frustration.

Childhood and Growing Up
The one thing that everyone knows about *Catcher* is Holden's fantasy of the rye field perched high on a cliff in which young children are playing. He sees himself as protecting the children from falling off the edge of the cliff by "catching" them if they are about to tumble over. It is a very beautiful symbol for Holden's desire to preserve the innocence of childhood and to protect them from the dangers of the world, but it is also a flawed image.

Children have to grow up; they have to take responsibility for their own safety; it is only by taking risks that they learn. Even more fundamentally, as Phoebe points out, Holden's image is based on his having misheard the lyric to "Comin' Thro' the Rye" by Robert Burns. The key line is not, "If a body *catch* a body comin' through the rye," but, "If a body *meet* a body, coming through the rye." The word 'meet' is actually a euphemism for 'have sex with,' which could not be further away from Holden's image of preserving indefinitely the innocence of childhood. That wonderful symbol is based on a complete misunderstanding of the transitory nature of childhood.

Human Mortality

People die, and when someone close to you dies (and this has happened twice to Holden) it is very painful. Never allowing anyone ever to get close to you is not, however, the solution. Suicide often appears to be an attractive option to Holden, a sure sign that he is on the wrong track.

The Catcher in the Rye by J.D.Salinger
Guiding Questions
How to use this study guide:
This novel deserves to be read reflectively. These questions are designed to help you to locate and to understand characters, settings, and themes in the text. They do not normally have simple answers, nor is there always one answer. Consider a range of possible interpretations - preferably by discussing the questions with others. Disagreement is to be encouraged!

Chapter 1
In a **first person narrative,** the reader begins blind; that is, we know nothing about the speaker/writer whose **voice** we hear. There are four different aspects of the narrator which the reader needs to learn about: character/personality, background history, current situation, reliability. The first chapter tells the reader most about the narrator's character. Although he explicitly refuses to go into his biography, inevitably details emerge piece by piece. It is his current situation, and how he got into it, that the narrator identifies as his chief concern. The reader comes to understand that Holden is an **unreliable narrator**. Whilst he sees the faults in others with 20/20 vision, he appears to be blind to the fact that he is quite capable of the same faults which he finds so objectionable in others. Add to this the fact that he is a self-confessed "terrific liar" (22)!

1. Character/personality:
- The narrator's use of language is, to say the least, distinctive. What clues does it give you to his character? [Note that 'bad language' is one of the reasons most often cited by those who wish to ban this book. Actually, the language appears pretty tame today, but just imagine the reaction it got in 1945!]
- The narrator's attitude to 'generally respected' institutions and groups is also distinctive. What is his attitude to Hollywood, Pencey Prep, and the fencing team? [Did I miss anything?] What clues does it give you to his character?

2. Background history:
- What do we learn of the narrator's family members and of his feeling for them?

3. Current situation:
- The narrator says he is "out here" (3). What clues does the reader get as to where he might be and why he might be there?

4. Reliability:
- What indications do you find in this chapter that the reader should not accept the truth of everything Holden says?

Notes:
All "that David Copperfield kind of crap" (3). Here is the opening of Dickens' novel so that you can see the kind of writing that the narrator is reacting against:

A Study Guide

Chapter One; I Am Born

Whether I shall turn out to be the hero of my own life, or whether that station will be held by anybody else, these pages must show. To begin my life with the beginning of my life, I record that I was born (as I have been informed and believe) on a Friday, at twelve o'clock at night. It was remarked that the clock began to strike, and I began to cry, simultaneously.

In consideration of the day and hour of my birth, it was declared by the nurse, and by some sage women in the neighbourhood who had taken a lively interest in me several months before there was any possibility of our becoming personally acquainted, first, that I was destined to be unlucky in life; and secondly, that I was privileged to see ghosts and spirits; both these gifts inevitably attaching, as they believed, to all unlucky infants of either gender, born towards the small hours on a Friday night.

I need say nothing here, on the first head, because nothing can show better than my history whether that prediction was verified or falsified by the result. On the second branch of the question, I will only remark, that unless I ran through that part of my inheritance while I was still a baby, I have not come into it yet. But I do not at all complain of having been kept out of this property; and if anybody else should be in the present enjoyment of it, he is heartily welcome to keep it.

I was born with a caul, which was advertised for sale, in the newspapers, at the low price of fifteen guineas. Whether sea-going people were short of money about that time, or were short of faith and preferred cork jackets, I don't know; all I know is, that there was but one solitary bidding, and that was from an attorney connected with the bill-broking business, who offered two pounds in cash, and the balance in sherry, but declined to be guaranteed from drowning on any higher bargain. Consequently the advertisement was withdrawn at a dead loss—for as to sherry, my poor dear mother's own sherry was in the market then—and ten years afterwards, the caul was put up in a raffle down in our part of the country, to fifty members at half-a-crown a head, the winner to spend five shillings. I was present myself, and I remember to have felt quite uncomfortable and confused, at a part of myself being disposed of in that way. The caul was won, I recollect, by an old lady with a hand-basket, who, very reluctantly, produced from it the stipulated five shillings, all in halfpence, and twopence halfpenny short—as it took an immense time and a great waste of arithmetic, to endeavour without any effect to prove to her. It is a fact which will be long remembered as remarkable down there, that she was never drowned, but died triumphantly in bed, at ninety-two. I have understood that it was, to the last, her proudest boast,

The Catcher in the Rye by J.D.Salinger

that she never had been on the water in her life, except upon a bridge; and that over her tea (to which she was extremely partial) she, to the last, expressed her indignation at the impiety of mariners and others, who had the presumption to go "meandering" about the world. It was in vain to represent to her that some conveniences, tea perhaps included, resulted from this objectionable practice. She always returned, with greater emphasis and with an instinctive knowledge of the strength of her objection, "Let us have no meandering."

Not to meander myself, at present, I will go back to my birth.

I was born at Blunderstone, in Suffolk, or 'there by', as they say in Scotland. I was a posthumous child. My father's eyes had closed upon the light of this world six months, when mine opened on it. There is something strange to me, even now, in the reflection that he never saw me; and something stranger yet in the shadowy remembrance that I have of my first childish associations with his white grave-stone in the churchyard, and of the indefinable compassion I used to feel for it lying out alone there in the dark night, when our little parlour was warm and bright with fire and candle, and the doors of our house were—almost cruelly, it seemed to me sometimes—bolted and locked against it...

If you read the Dickens extract carefully, you will have noted this sentence, "I was born with a caul ...," and you may have noted the similarity with Holden's surname *Caul*field. Here is a definition, "A caul or cowl (Latin: Caput galeatum, literally, 'helmeted head') is a piece of membrane that can cover a newborn's head and face. Birth with a caul is rare, occurring in fewer than 1 in 80,000 births. The caul is harmless and is immediately removed by the physician or midwife upon delivery of the child" (Wikipedia). It has been suggested that the narrator's name is a pun (play on words): 'hold onto the caul.' This makes a lot of sense because Holden is trying to hold onto the safe, restricted view of the world that he had as a child.

Chapter 2

This chapter fills in information about why the narrator (now identified as Holden Caulfield, 16 years old at the time of the story and 17 years old now) left Pencey Prep.

5. Make a list of the things about Mr. Spencer which really irritate Holden. Given that this is quite a long list, what is it about this teacher that makes Holden want to visit him to say goodbye?

6. Holden hates things and people which he considers 'phony' - it is one of his favorite words! Explain why he thinks of each of the following as 'phony': "Life being like a game" (12), the word "Grand" (14), Elkton Hills in general, and the principal, Mr. Haas, in particular (19).

7. Despite condemning what he finds 'phony,' Holden says many things to Mr. Spencer which are 'phony.' Give examples. How do you explain his hypocrisy?

A Study Guide

Chapter 3

The red hunting hat is frequently seen as an important **symbol** in the novel. It certainly represents Holden's individuality. Throughout the novel it will protect Holden, rather like a replacement caul.

8. Holden describes himself as "quite illiterate, but I read a lot" (24). This seems to be a **paradox**. What is he saying about himself?

Notes:
Isak Dinesen was one of the pen names of Danish author Karen von Blixen-Finecke (17 April 1885 – 7 September 1962). *Out of Africa* (1937) is her account of living for seventeen years in Kenya.

Ringgold Wilmer Lardner (March 6, 1885 – September 25, 1933) was an American sports writer whose short stories were very popular. The specific story to which Holden refers is called "There Are Smiles."

Thomas Hardy (2 June 1840 – 11 January 1928) was a popular English novelist and poet known for the harsh realism of his Wessex Tales. *The Return of the Native* (1878) tells the story of Diggory Venn's tragic love for the "deeply flawed heroine" Eustacia Vye (Wikipedia).

William Somerset Maugham (25 January 1874 – 16 December 1965) was a very successful English playwright, novelist and short story writer. *Of Human Bondage* (1915) tells the story of the orphan Philip Carey who is born with a club foot. After various disastrous relationships and career decisions, Phillip finds some happiness in both his personal and professional life.

Chapter 4

9. Holden seems to like his roommate Stradlater more than Ackley, but he does not like Stradlater much. Make a list of the things he has against him.
10. Describe Holden's feelings about (for?) Jane Gallagher. Why do you think that he does not go down to see her?

Notes:
"Song of India" is an aria from Rimsky-Korsakov's opera *Sadko* (1896) which Tommy Dorsey did an instrumental jazz arrangement of in 1938.

"Slaughter on Tenth Avenue" is ballet music by Richard Rodgers in the Broadway musical comedy *On Your Toes* (1936).

Chapter 5

Holden's essay on his brother's baseball glove gives a lot of insight into his (unacknowledged) psychological problems. That glove is also related to his later vision of himself as 'the catcher in the rye.'

11. In case you have not yet noticed it, Holden (foul-mouthed Holden) is incredibly sensitive to beauty. Give some examples.
12. In terms of explaining how he comes to be "out here" (3), this chapter gives the first real clues. Explain.

The Catcher in the Rye by J.D.Salinger

Chapter 6
Throughout the novel, Holden gets angry with just about everyone (he even despises his brother for selling out to Hollywood and finds his sister Phoebe too demonstrative). What he is actually doing is projecting his own unhappiness onto others.
13. Explain Holden's angry outburst against Stradlater.

Chapter 7
14. Holden uses the word "lonesome" to describe his feelings after the fight with Stradlater, which is perhaps a little unexpected. Explain how this feeling originates and how it explains his impulsive decision to leave Pencey Prep.

Chapter 8
15. Holden has already told us (boasted?) that he is "the most terrific liar you ever saw in your life" (22) and his conversation on the train with Mrs. Morrow provides plenty of proof of this. The lies themselves are less interesting than understanding why he tells them. What is your explanation?

Chapter 9
In the Edmont Hotel, Holden comes face-to-face with adult sexuality in forms that he finds 'perverted' and 'crummy' from a man cross-dressing, to obviously gay men, and a couple who seem turned on by spitting their drinks in each other's faces. Holden's problem is that, throughout the narrative, he has an idealized vision of sex as being a tremendously meaningful act between two people who care deeply for each other. Reality does not conform to his vision.
16. How does this chapter illustrate Holden's contradictory attitude to girls/women?

Chapter 10
For someone who despises everyone he meets, Holden appears desperate to meet people - particularly women. Put simply, he is lonely.
17. Describe Holden's feeling for his sister Phoebe.
18. What is it that Holden despises about all of the women he sees in the hotel that night? Why does he attach himself to the three women at the club and particularly to the blond?

Notes:
Peter Lorre and **Gary Cooper** were movie stars.
The Jitterbug was an uninhibited dance style in the Swing Era (1935-1946).
The Stork Club and **El Morocco** were nightclubs in New York City which during the 1930s, 40s and 50s attracted celebrities and other elites.
The Radio City Music Hall, opened in 1932, remains one of the top tourist attractions in New York.

A Study Guide

Chapter 11
Holden regards his relationship with Jane Gallagher as having been just about perfect. He felt an emotional connection to her which enabled him to offer her love and support when she was unhappy without any of the complications of teenage sexuality.
19. Why does Holden feel so protective towards Jane Gallagher?

Chapter 12
The word "lonesome" occurs twice on page 106, and Holden says that he feels "depressed" (106, 110). Holden's problem appears to be that he feels a desperate need to have people around him but his social interactions convince him that, "People are always ruining things for you" (114).
20. Briefly explain what Holden finds 'phony' about Ernie, Lillian Simmons, and the Navy guy she is with.

Chapter 13
"Depressed" is a word that comes up a lot in this chapter: thinking about his stolen gloves and his being "yellow" (117); standing in his hotel lobby, he feels "Depressed and all. I almost wished I was dead" (118); and being with the prostitute makes him feel "more depressed than sexy ... *She* was depressing" (125). [Did I miss any?]
21. Why does Holden get himself into the "big mess" (118) with the prostitute Sunny?

Notes:
Monsieur Blanchard is a fictional character: a rich Frenchman who is very attractive to women. The character, who lives in Monte Carlo, appears in the story "Orinsi, the Croupier" included in the anthology *Warped in the Making: Crimes of Love and Hate* (1927) by the prolific crime-writer H Ashton-Wolfe (1881-1959).

Chapter 14
This chapter begins with Holden feeling "miserable ... so depressed, you can't imagine" (129) and ends with him saying, "What I really felt like, though, was committing suicide" (136). For the second time in around twelve hours, he seems almost deliberately to get himself beaten up.
22. What incident in Holden's childhood helps to explain his recurring loneliness and depression?

Chapter 15
Surprisingly, one of the most disconcerting social interactions that Holden has is with the two nuns eating breakfast. The trouble is that they do not conform to Holden's stereotypes. They are well-meaning adults who are not phonies; they are Catholics who do not talk about religion; they are teachers who seem to love

The Catcher in the Rye by J.D.Salinger

teaching. One of them (unlike Holden himself) even has no problems with the sexual aspects of *Romeo and Juliet*. All very confusing!

23. Holden explains about how his having good suitcases and his room mate having cheap ones ruined his relationship with Dick Slagle. Later, he explains that he feels Catholics always want to know if you are Catholic and how this almost ruined his relationship with Louis Shaney. At the end of the chapter, Holden says of the Catholic thing, "It's just like those suitcases I was telling you about. In a way" (147). In what way?

24. Examine closely what Holden says about his reactions to *Romeo and Juliet*. What light does this shed on Holden's situation?

Chapter 16

Two things make Holden feel much better in this chapter: the little boy walking in the street singing (150) and the polite little girl he meets in the park (155).

25. Why do you think that Holden does not go into the Museum of Natural History after having walked so far to get to it? [The following quotations may help: "The best thing, though, in that museum was that everything always stayed right where it was" (157); "The only thing that would be different would be *you* ... I mean you'd be *different* in some way - I can't explain what I mean. And even if I could, I'm not sure I'd feel like it" (158); "they didn't want me around, so I let them alone" (159).]

Notes:

Estelle Fletcher (1928-2005) was a real singer, but never recorded the song *Little Shirley Beans*. Holden says that the record is "very old," so Fletcher would have been a child when she is supposed to have recorded it. The record Holden buys would have been a 78 rpm shellac gramophone record.

If a Body Catch a Body is based on a traditional children's song which derives from the poem "Comin' Thro' the Rye" written in 1782 by Robert Burns (1759–1796). Holden misinterprets a part of this poem to mean, "If a body catch a body" rather than, "If a body meet a body / Comin' thro' the rye." The original poem is also full of sexual references (it asks whether it is wrong for a man and a woman who happen to meet in the fields to have sexual relations even though they have no relationship) which Holden also appears to be unaware of.

Sir Laurence Olivier adapted, directed, and starring in the 1948 British film *Hamlet*.

Alfred Lunt and his wife **Lynn Fontanne** were, from the 1930s, one of the most famous acting couples in America. *I Know My Love* was a play by S. N. Behrman which ran for one season (1949-50) on Broadway. This places action of the novel in December 1949.

Chapter 17

Holden tries to explain his sense of alienation to Sally Hayes. He tells her, "'I don't get hardly anything out of anything. I'm in bad shape. I'm in *lousy* shape'"

(171). Sally is, however, incapable of offering him the love and compassion that he needs.

26. Why does Holden's idea of he and Sally running away together cause a bitter quarrel between them?

Chapter 18
Holden mentions many times how much he hates movies because he finds them 'phony.' He similarly dismisses Ernest Hemingway's *A Farewell to Arms* (1929) as "a phony" (182), though F. Scott Fitzgerald's *The Great Gatsby* (1925) he likes.

27. Why does Holden suppose that his older brother D. B. "hated the Army worse than the war"?

Chapter 19
28. Holden calls Carl Luce mainly because he cannot think of anyone else to call. Why does Holden keep making appointments with people whom he does not like, people he actually despises?

29. In their conversation, what is it that he is trying to learn from Luce?

Chapter 20
Having been worried about the ducks on the pond in the Park, Holden finally decides to go there. Although he has not understood it, he has been worried about the disappearance of the ducks because it **symbolizes** the impermanence of the real world. His brother Allie (another pun perhaps for 'ally' or friend) also disappeared, and so has Jane because she now seems to be a sexually active teen.

30. You will not be surprised that the breaking of the record which he bought for Phoebe is seen to be deeply **symbolic**. What do you think that it may be intended by the author to **symbolize**?

Chapter 21
Holden's visit to his parents' apartment is the beginning of the **climax** of the novel. Unfortunately, Phoebe appears to be in many ways much more mature than he is and this begins a confrontation with reality which might finally save Holden.

31. The last sentence of the chapter is, "I was all out" (215). Comment on the possible significances of this sentence.

Chapter 22
Students frequently have problems grasping what a **symbol** is in literature, and the usual definition, "A symbol is a person, place, or thing used by the writer to represent an abstract idea or concept; a symbol stands for something beyond itself," does not help them much. However, Holden's description of his wish to be 'the catcher in the rye' (224-5) really exemplifies what a symbol is.

32. The **climax** of this chapter is when Phoebe tells Holden the truth about

The Catcher in the Rye by J.D.Salinger

himself. Quote the devastating truth that she states.
33. As Phoebe points out, Holden's wish to be 'the catcher in the rye' is based on his misunderstanding of the words of the song (224). What significance do you find in the fact that Holden's vision is based on an error and that it is Phoebe (six years younger than her brother) who points this out? Explain.

Chapter 23
34. Why does Holden cry?

Chapter 24
In this chapter, Holden literally runs out of people to trust. Everyone (except Phoebe) in the book seems to have let him down. Ironically, Mr. Antolini sees Holden as falling and is desperately trying to save him, but he is not trying to keep Holden in his safe cocoon of childhood, he is trying to get him to operate in the real world.
35. In what ways is Mr. Antolini's view of education different from the view to which Holden has been subjected in every school he has attended and by every teacher (including Mr. Spencer)?
36. Is Holden right to suspect Mr. Antolini of making a sexual advance? [Recall Holden's earlier reactions to homosexuals in his hotel and his fear that he might suddenly turn into a homosexual. Come to think of it, sitting there watching his little sister sleep, or covering Jane's face with kisses, could be viewed as quite kinky, but that would not mean that it was.]

Chapter 25
Holden comes close to a complete mental breakdown in this chapter. He desperately tries to wipe out obscene graffiti, but soon comes to realize that there is just too much of it for him to cope with. Holden's plans to run away are, of course, completely unrealistic - even Phoebe can see that! Running away from reality is just the last of a series of ways Holden has attempted to deny the reality that he is soon going to be an adult and will have to live in a real world which is always short of ideal.
The vision of the catcher in the rye is here replaced by that of the children reaching for the ring. Critics often seem to underestimate the life-changing nature of this second vision. It embodies an entirely different way of looking at growing up.
37. Identify the stages of Holden's physical and mental disintegration.
38. In what ways does Holden revise his judgment of Mr. Antolini's actions of the night before? Why is this process important to his psychological development?
39. What is it that finally saves Holden's sanity? [Clue: Watching Phoebe on the carrousel, Holden has an epiphany (a sudden intuition or insight, a flash of understanding that has life-changing implications). What does he realize? Second clue: Explain the **symbolism** of the carrousel ring.]

Chapter 26
The ending of the novel is **ambiguous**: it is unclear to what extent Holden will change, will apply what he has learned.
40. Finally, we know where Holden is when he tells/writes his narrative and can reconstruct what happened to bring him there. Explain.

General Questions
1. Many times in his narrative Holden wants to contact Jane Gallagher. Why does he feel this urge so strongly? Why does he never do it?
2. Holden is a virgin who tries very hard to loose his virginity but fails utterly. Looking at the examples he gives (from fooling around on the back seats of cars to paying for a prostitute), explain why Holden is incapable of having sex in these circumstances.
3. Why on earth would anyone want to ban this book?

The Catcher in the Rye by J. D. Salinger Reading Quizzes

Reading Quizzes:

Chapters 1 - 4

Chapter 1
1. D. B. is Holden's:
    a. Younger brother;
    b. Father
    c. Elder brother
    d. Sister
2. One of D. B's early stories is called:
    a. The Secret Cave
    b. The Secret Friend
    c. The Secret Goldfish
3. Holden has just got back from a fencing meet in:
    a. Albany
    b. New York
    c. Scranton
    d. New Jersey
4. Holden goes to see Mr. Spencer:
    a. To discuss his history exam
    b. To say good-bye
    c. Because he is sick

Chapter 2
5. What expression does Mr. Spencer use that Holden hates because it is "a phony"?
    a. My boy
    b. Excellent
    c. Grand
    d. Son
6. What does Mr. Spencer do that Holden regards as a "dirty trick"?
    a. Gives him an F in history
    b. Makes him read his exam paper
    c. Asks what he would have done in his place
    d. Tells him he is trying to help
7. What are Mr. Spencer's final words to Holden?
    a. Good night
    b. Stay well
    c. Good luck
    d. Take care

A Study Guide

Chapter 3

8. At Pencey Prep, Holden lives in:
    a. Hapsburg Memorial Wing
    b. Ossenburger Memorial Wing
    c. Banburger Memorial Wing

9. When in New York, Holden had bought
    a. Brown hunting hat
    b. Blue hunting hat
    c. Red hunting hat
    d. Green hunting hat

10. Which of these novels does Holden not mention having read?
    a. *Heart of Darkness*
    b. *The Return of the Native*
    c. *Out of Africa*
    d. *Of Human Bondage*

11. Ackley irritates Holden by:
    a. Picking his nose
    b. Squeezing his spots
    c. Cutting his nails
    d. Talking about sex

12. Holden is reluctant to lend Stradlater his hound's-tooth jacket because:
    a. He might get it dirty
    b. He might not return it
    c. He might stretch it
    d. It was D. B's

Chapter 4

13. Stradlater asks Holden to write him an essay for English. The only requirement is that it has to:
    a. Be exciting
    b. Have lots of dialogue
    c. Be long
    d. Be very descriptive

14. When talking to Stradlater in the can, Holden does all of the following except:
    a. Tap-dances
    b. Whistles
    c. Puts Stradlater in a half nelson
    d. Asks about his date

The Catcher in the Rye by J. D. Salinger Reading Quizzes

15. Which of the following is not true of Jane Gallagher?
    a. Her parents are divorced
    b. She plays checkers
    c. She loves dancing
    d. She plays chess

Chapters 5 - 8

Chapter 5

1. Holden decides to spend Saturday evening seeing a movie which is strange because:
    a. He hates movies
    b. It is Ackley's idea
    c. He has no money
    d. He has a date
2. When he writes the essay for Stradlater, Holden describes:
    a. His bedroom
    b. His garage
    c. A baseball bat
    d. A baseball glove
3. Holden's brother Allie was:
    a. Two years older than him
    b. Two years younger than him
    c. The same age as him
4. Allie died:
    a. In a car accident
    b. Of leukemia
    c. Of meningitis
    d. Of tuberculosis
5. After Allie's death, Holden:
    a. Trashed the garage
    b. Trashed his room
    c. Trashed the car

Chapter 6

6. When Stradlater reads the essay Holden has written, which two of the following does he do?
    a. Tears it up
    b. Swears
    c. Gets angry at Holden
    d. Likes it

7. Holden asks Stradlater whether:
    a. He had a good date
    b. He had sex with his date
    c. He liked Jane Gallagher
8. Holden and Stradlater get into a fight. Who starts it?
    a. Stradlater
    b. Holden
9. Who wins the fight?
    a. Stradlater
    b. Holden

Chapter 7
10. After the fight, Holden goes to Ackley's room and asks him:
    a. To help him clean up
    b. If he can sleep there that night
    c. To help him get back at Stradlater
11. Before he leaves Pencey, Holden does all of the following except:
    a. Packs two Gladstone bags
    b. Sells his typewriter
    c. Throws out his ice skates

Chapter 8
12. The woman Holden meets on the train is the mother of fellow Pency student:
    a. Ted Morrow
    b. Lou Morrow
    c. Ernest Morrow
    d. Peter Morrow
13. Holden tells her that her son:
    a. Got elected class president
    b. Has a very original personality
    c. Is his best friend
14. Another of the lies that Holden tells the woman is that he was called home because:
    a. Of a family emergency
    b. His father is in hospital
    c. He needs an operation

Chapters 9 - 12
Chapter 9
1. Holden asks his cab driver about the duck on the lagoon in Central Park:
    a. East
    b. West
    c. North
    d. South

The Catcher in the Rye by J. D. Salinger Reading Quizzes

2. The hotel into which Holden checks is:
    a. The Hilton
    b. The Edmont
    c. The Raddison
    d. The Belmont
3. Which of the following does Holden not see from his hotel window?
    a. a man and woman spitting at each other
    b. a man dressing as a woman
    c. two men kissing
4. Holden rings a woman whose number a guy from Princeton had given him. Her name is:
    a. Faith Bonner
    b. Faith Raymond
    c. Faith Boyle
    d. Faith Cavendish

Chapter 10

5. Phoebe's favorite movie is:
    a. *The Baker's Wife*
    b. *The Birds*
    c. *The 39 Steps*
    d. *Snow White*
6. Holden goes into the Lavender Room where he joins three women. He calls them:
    a. Plain
    b. Ugly
    c. Attractive
    d. Talkative
7. Although he dances with all three women, Holden is most attracted to:
    a. The blond
    b. The brunette
    c. The redhead
8. Holden tells one of the girls that he has just seen the movie star:
    a. Kirk Douglas
    b. Randolph Scott
    c. Gary Cooper
    d. Tyrone Power

Chapter 11

9 The time Holden kisses Jane Gallagher they are:
    a. Playing checkers
    b. In the cinema
    c. In the back of a car

10. He kisses her because:
    a. They are on a date
    b. She asks him too
    c. She is crying
    d. He wants sex with her
11. The main form of physical contact that Holden has with Jane is:
    a. Kissing
    b. Cuddling
    c. Holding hands
12. Holden decides to go to a nightclub in Greenwich Village called:
    a. Erole's
    b. Eddie's
    c. Ernie's
    d. Emanuel's

Chapter 12

13. On the way to Greenwich Village, Holden has an argument with the cab-driver about:
    a. The fair
    b. The time
    c. The speed
    d. The ducks
14. In the nightclub, Holden meets an old girlfriend of his brother, Lillian Simmons, who asks Holden to join her. What does he do?
    a. He joins her
    b. He has an argument with the man she's with
    c. He makes an excuse and leaves
    d. He kisses her

Chapters 13 - 16

Chapter 13

1. How does Holden get back to his hotel?
    a. He takes a cab
    b. He rides the subway
    c. He catches a bus
    d. He walks
2. When he gets back, the elevator man offers to get him a prostitute. His name is:
    a. Maurice
    b. Harry
    c. Pauly
    d. Reggie

The Catcher in the Rye by J. D. Salinger Reading Quizzes

3. Holden explains his still being a virgin to the reader. He says that:
    a. Girls scare him
    b. He is not interested in sex
    c. When a girl says no, he stops
4. When the prostitute comes on to him, Holden tells her:
    a. He wants to talk
    b. He is recovering from an operation
    c. He doesn't feel like himself
    d. All three of these

Chapter 14
5. The name of the young prostitute who comes to Holden's hotel room is:
    a. Honey
    b. Bunny
    c. Boney
    d. Sunny
6. When Holden goes to bed, he tries unsuccessfully:
    a. To pray
    b. To stop being depressed
    c. To feel miserable
7. How much does the elevator man insist that Holden owes the prostitute?
    a. Five dollars
    b. Ten dollars
    c. Fifteen dollars
    d. Twenty dollars
8. Where does the elevator man hit Holden?
    a. His back
    b. His chest
    c. His arm
    d. His stomach

Chapter 15
9. After a brief sleep, Holden calls and makes a date with:
    a. Sally Dayes
    b. Sally Hayes
    c. Sally Mayes
    d. Sally Bayes
10. Over breakfast, Holden talks with two nuns. Which of these texts do they not discuss?
    a. *The Great Gatsby*
    b. *The Return of the Native*
    c. *Romeo and Juliet*

11. Holden makes a contribution to the nuns of:
    a. Five dollars
    b. Ten dollars
    c. Fifteen dollars
    d. Twenty dollars

Chapter 16

12. What is the title of the record that Holden buys for Phoebe?
    a. Little Red Riding Hood
    b. Little Shirley Temple
    c. Little Shirley Beans

13. For his date, Holden buys two theater tickets for:
    a. *I Know My Love*
    b. *I Know My Girl*
    c. *I Know My Way*

14. Holden meets a "polite' little kid" in the park who knows Phoebe. He helps the kid to:
    a. Take off her skates
    b. Put on her skates
    c. Tighten her skates
    d. Find her skates

15. Holden likes going to the Museum of Natural History because:
    a. It always has something new
    b. It is always exactly the same
    c. It is always different
    d. He always feels the same there

Chapters 17 - 20

Chapter 17

1. The stars of the play Holden sees with his date are a man and wife couple called:
    a. The Bunts
    b. The Lunts
    c. The Hunts
    d. The Munts

2. After the theatre, Holden agrees to take his date to:
    a. Central Park
    b. Broadway
    c. Radio City
    d. The Empire State Building

The Catcher in the Rye by J. D. Salinger Reading Quizzes

3. At the end of their date, the two have an argument because:
    a. Holden refuses to come round Christmas Eve to help trim the tree
    b. Holden wants them to run away together
    c. Holden talks about Jane Gallagher
    d. Holden tells her he has been kicked out of school

Chapter 18
4. Holden rings Carl Luce, but has time to kill before they can meet so he:
    a. Takes a walk in Central Park
    b. Goes to another play
    c. Goes to see a movie
5. Holden agrees to meet Carl in:
    a. The City Bar
    b. The Tatlers' Bar
    c. The Wiki Bar
    d. The Wicker Bar
6. Which of the following novels does Holden prefer?
    a. *The Great Gatsby*
    b. *A Farewell to Arms*

Chapter 19
7. When Holden meets Carl, he mainly quizzes him about:
    a. Life at Columbia
    b. Football
    c. His sex life
    d. His grades
8. Carl's father is :
    a. A professor
    b. A teacher
    c. A dentist
    d. A psychiatrist
9. Which statement about Carl's girlfriend is not true? She is:
    a. Living in Queens
    b. Older than Carl
    c. A sculptress
    d. Chinese

Chapter 20
10. Holden gets drunk. Which of the following does he try (unsuccessfully) to call on the phone?
    a. Jane Gallagher
    b. Sally Hayes
    c. Faith Cavendish
    d. Phoebe Caulfield

A Study Guide

11. Holden takes a walk to the park. He has just got there when something terrible happens. He:
    a. Breaks Phoebe's record
    b. Meets his father
    c. Loses his money
    d. Is mugged

12. It is very cold in the park, so Holden decides:
    a. To return to his hotel
    b. To go to a movie
    c. To go home
    d. To go to a bar

Chapters 21 - 23

Chapter 21

1. In the apartment building, Holden lies to:
    a. The caretaker
    b. The maid
    c. The night clerk
    d. The elevator boy

2. When Holden goes into Phoebe's room which of the following does he not do?
    a. Reads her notebook
    b. Watches her lying asleep
    c. Wakes her up at once

3. What part is Phoebe playing in the Christmas Pageant that she wants Holden to come and see?
    a. George Washington
    b. Thomas Jefferson
    c. Horatio Gates
    d. Benedict Arnold

4. What does Phoebe say when she understands that Holden has got kicked out of school?
    a. Mom'll kill you!
    b. D. B'll kill you!
    c. I'll kill you!
    d. Dad'll kill you!

Chapter 22

5. Which of the following does Phoebe not say?
    a. Why do you do it?
    b. I suppose you only passed English
    c. Don't swear so much
    d. Name something you'd like to be

The Catcher in the Rye by J. D. Salinger Reading Quizzes

6. Asked to name one thing he likes a lot, Holden replies:
    a. D. B.
    b. Jane Gallagher
    c. The Natural History Museum
    d. Allie
7. Phoebe tells Holden that she is taking lessons in:
    a. Belching
    b. Ballet
    c. Skating
    d. Writing stories
8. Which are the correct words of the song Holden has in his head?
    a. If a body meet a body coming through the rye
    b. If a body catch a body coming through the rye
9. At the start of this chapter, Holden:
    a. Plays checkers with Phoebe
    b. Dances with Phoebe
    c. Reads Phoebe a story
    d. Reads Phoebe's notebook
10. Phoebe believes that she can:
    a. Make herself feverish at will
    b. Make herself calm at will
    c. Make herself cold at will
11. Before he leaves, Holden does all of the following except:
    a. Borrows money from Phoebe
    b. Cries uncontrollably
    c. Lies about where he's going

Chapters 24 - 26
Chapter 24
1. Mr. and Mrs. Antolini live in:
    a. A modest apartment
    b. A town house
    c. A swanky apartment
    d. A hotel
2. Their home is:
    a. Immaculate
    b. Tidy
    c Rather untidy
    d. Extremely untidy
3. Mr. Antolini say that he has a feeling that Holden is:
    a. Going to be a great writer
    b. Heading for a terrible fall
    c. Being unreasonable

A Study Guide

4. Holden leaves the flat because Mr. Antolini:
    a. Takes his father's side
    b. Is still in his underwear
    c. Pats him on the head while he sleeps
    d. Says he has to get to bed

Chapter 25
5. Which of these statements about James Castle is not true:
    a. He jumped from a window
    b. Holden knew him well
    c. He was wearing Holden's sweater
    d. He was being bullied
6. Holden reads a magazine article that convinces him that he:
    a. Has cancer
    b. Has an ulcer
    c. Has diabetes
    d. Has a spinal problem
7. How does Holden arrange to meet Phoebe?
    a. Sends a message home
    b. Calls home
    c. He goes to her school
    d. Goes home
8. When Phoebe meets Holden, she brings:
    a. Her parents
    b. Her friend
    c. Her suitcase
    d. Her record
9. Holden takes Phoebe where for the afternoon?
    a. The cinema
    b. The theatre
    c. Back to school
    d. The zoo
10. What does Phoebe do on the carousel?
    a. She's the only child who reaches for the ring
    b. She reaches for the ring like all the others

Chapter 26
11. What word best describes the ending of the novel?
    a. Ambivalent
    b Positive
    c. Depressing
    d. Ambiguous

Catcher in the Rye by J.D. Salinger
Reading Quizzes: The Answers
Reading Quiz: Chapters 1 - 4
1. D. B. is Holden's: *c. Elder brother*
2. One of D. B's early stories is called: *c. The Secret Goldfish*
3. Holden has just got back from a fencing meet in: *b. New York*
4. Holden goes to see Mr. Spencer: *b. To say good-bye*
5. What expression does Mr. Spencer use that Holden hates because it is "a phony"? *c. Grand*
6. What does Mr. Spencer do that Holden regards as a "dirty trick"? *b. Makes him read his exam paper*
7. What are Mr. Spencer's final words to Holden? *c. Good luck*
8. At Pencey Prep, Holden lives in: *b. Ossenburger Memorial Wing*
9. When in New York, Holden had bought: *c. A red hunting hat*
10. Which of these novels does Holden not mention having read? *a. 'Heart of Darkness'*
11. Ackley irritates Holden by: *c. Cutting his nails*
12. Holden is reluctant to lend Stradlater his hound's-tooth jacket because: *c. He might stretch it*
13. Stradlater asks Holden to write him an essay for English. The only requirement is that it has to: *d. Be very descriptive*
14. When talking to Stradlater in the can, Holden does all of the following except: *b. Whistles*
15. Which of the following is not true of Jane Gallagher? *d. She plays chess*

Reading Quiz: Chapters 5 - 8
1. Holden decides to spend Saturday evening seeing a movie which is strange because: *a. He hates movies*
2. When he writes the essay for Stradlater, Holden describes: *d. A baseball glove*
3. Holden's brother Allie was: *b. Two years younger than him*
4. Allie died: *b. Of leukemia*
5. After Allie's death, Holden: *a. Trashed the garage*
6. When Stradlater reads the essay Holden has written, which two of the following does he do? *b. Swears c. Gets angry at Holden*
7. Holden asks Stradlater whether: *b. He had sex with his date*
8. Holden and Stradlater get into a fight. Who starts it? *b. Holden*
9. Who wins the fight? *a. Stradlater*
10. After the fight, Holden goes to Ackley's room and asks him: *b. If he can sleep there that night*
11. Before he leaves Pencey, Holden does all of the following except: *c. Throws out his ice skates*
12. The woman Holden meets on the train is the mother of fellow Pencey student: *c. Ernest Morrow*

A Study Guide

13. Holden tells her that her son: *b. Has a very original personality*
14. Another lie that Holden tells the woman is that he was called home because: *c. He needs an operation*

Reading Quiz: Chapters 9 - 12

1. Holden asks his cab driver about the duck on the lagoon in Central Park: *d. South*
2. The hotel into which Holden checks is: *b. The Edmont*
3. Which of the following does Holden not see from his hotel window? *c. two men kissing*
4. Holden rings a woman whose number a guy from Princeton had given him. Her name is: *d. Faith Cavendish*
5. Phoebe's favorite movie is: c. *'The 39 Steps'*
6. Holden goes into the Lavender Room where he joins three women at their table. He calls them all: *b. Ugly*
7. Although he dances with all three women, Holden is most attracted to: *a. The blond*
8. Holden tells one of the girls that he has just seen the movie star: *c. Gary Cooper*
9. The time Holden kisses Jane Gallagher they are: *a. Playing checkers*
10. He kisses her because: *c. She is crying*
11. The main form of physical contact that Holden has with Jane is: *c. Holding hands*
12. Holden decides to go to a nightclub in Greenwich Village called: *c. Ernie's*
13. On the way to Greenwich Village, Holden has an argument with the cab-driver about: *d. The ducks*
14. In the nightclub, Holden meets and old girlfriend of his brother. Lillian Simmons asks Holden to join her. What does he do? *c. He makes an excuse and leaves*

Reading Quiz: Chapters 13 - 16

1. How does Holden get back to his hotel? *d. He walks*
2. When he gets back, the elevator man offers to get him a prostitute. His name is: *a. Maurice*
3. Holden explains his still being a virgin to the reader. He says that: *c. When a girl says no, he stops*
4. When the prostitute comes on to him, Holden tells her: *d. All three of these*
5. The name of the young prostitute who comes to Holden's hotel room is: *d. Sunny*
6. When Holden goes to bed, he tries unsuccessfully: *a. To pray*
7. How much does the elevator man insist that Holden owes the prostitute? *a. Five dollars*
8. Where does the elevator man hit Holden? *d. His stomach*
9. After a brief sleep, Holden calls and makes a movie date with: *b. Sally Hayes*

Catcher in the Rye by J.D. Salinger

10. Over breakfast, Holden talks with two nuns. Which of these texts do they not discuss? *a. 'The Great Gatsby'*
11. Holden makes a contribution to the nuns of: *b. Ten dollars*
12. What is the title of the record that Holden buys for Phoebe? *c. Little Shirley Beans*
13. For his date, Holden buys two theater tickets for: *a. 'I Know My Love'*
14. Holden meets a "polite little kid" in the park who knows Phoebe. He helps the kid to: *c. Tighten her skates*
15. Holden likes going to the Museum of Natural History because: *b. It is always exactly the same*

Reading Quiz: Chapters 17 - 20
1. The stars of the play Holden sees with his date are: *b. The Lunts*
2. After the theatre, Holden agrees to take his date to: *c. Radio City*
3. At the end of their date, the two have an argument because: *b. Holden wants them to run away together*
4. Holden rings Carl Luce, but has time to kill before they can meet so he: *c. Goes to see a movie*
5. Holden agrees to meet Carl in: *d. The Wicker Bar*
6. Which of the following novels does Holden prefer? *a. 'The Great Gatsby'*
7. When Holden meets Carl, he mainly quizzes him about: *c. His sex life*
8. Carl's father is : *d. A psychiatrist*
9. Which statement about Carl's girlfriend is not true? She is: *a. Living in Queens*
10. Holden gets drunk. Which of the following does he try (unsuccessfully) to call on the phone? *b. Sally Hayes*
11. Holden takes a walk to the park. He has just got there when something terrible happens. He: *a. Breaks Phoebe's record*
12. It is very cold in the park, so Holden decides: *c. To go home*

Reading Quiz: Chapters 21 - 23
1. In the apartment building, Holden lies to: *d. The elevator boy*
2. When Holden goes into Phoebe's room which of the following does he not do? *c. Wakes her up at once*
3. What part is Phoebe playing in the Christmas Pageant that she wants Holden to come and see? *d. Benedict Arnold*
4. What does Phoebe say when she understands that Holden has got kicked out of school? *d. Dad'll kill you!*
5. Which of the following does Phoebe not say? *b. I suppose you only passed English*
6. Asked to name one thing he likes a lot, Holden replies: *d. Allie*
7. Phoebe tells Holden that she is taking lessons in: *a. Belching*
8. Which are the correct words of the song Holden has in his head: *a. If a body meet a body coming through the rye*
9. At the start of this chapter, Holden: *b. Dances with Phoebe*

10. Phoebe believes that she can: *a. Make herself feverish at will*
11. Before he leaves, Holden does all of the following except: *c. Lies about where he's going*

Reading Quiz: Chapters 24 - 26
12. Mr. and Mrs. Antolini live in: *c. A swanky apartment*
2. Their home is: *d. extremely untidy*
3. Mr. Antolini say that he has a feeling that Holden is: *b. Heading for a terrible fall*
4. Holden leaves the flat because Mr. Antolini: *c. Pats him on the head while he sleeps*
5. Which of these statements about James Castle is not true: *b. Holden knew him well*
6. Holden reads a magazine article that convinces him that he: *a. Has cancer*
7. How does Holden arrange to meet Phoebe? *c. He goes to her school*
8. When Phoebe meets Holden, she brings: *c. Her suitcase*
9. Holden takes Phoebe where for the afternoon? *d. The zoo*
10. What does Phoebe do on the carousel? *b. She reaches for the ring like all the others*
11. What word best describes the ending of the novel? *d. Ambiguous*

Catcher in the Rye by J.D. Salinger
Literary terms

Ambiguous, ambiguity: when a statement is unclear in meaning – ambiguity may be deliberate or accidental.

Analogy: a comparison which treats two things as identical in one or more specified ways.

Antagonist: a character or force opposing the protagonist.

Antithesis: the complete opposite of something.

Climax: the conflict to which the action has been building since the start of the play or story.

Colloquialism: the casual, informal mainly spoken language of ordinary people – often called "slang."

Connotation: the ideas, feelings and associations generated by a word or phrase.

Dark comedy: comedy which has a serious implication – comedy that deals with subjects not usually treated humorously (e.g., death).

Dialogue: a conversation between two or more people in direct speech.

Diction: the writer's choice of words in order to create a particular effect.

Equivocation: saying something which is capable of two interpretations with the intention of misrepresenting the truth.

Euphemism: a polite word for an ugly truth – for example, a person is said to be sleeping when they are actually dead.

Fallacy: a misconception resulting from incorrect reasoning.

First person: first person singular is "I" and plural is "we".

Foreshadowing: a statement or action which gives the reader a hint of what is likely to happen later in the narrative.

Genre: the type of literature into which a particular text falls (e.g. drama, poetry, novel).

Image, imagery: figurative language such as simile, metaphor, personification etc., or a description which conjures up a particularly vivid picture.

Imply, implication: when the text suggests to the reader a meaning which it does not actually state.

Infer, inference: the reader's act of going beyond what is stated in the text to draw conclusions.

Irony, ironic: a form of humor which undercuts the apparent meaning of a statement:

Conscious irony: irony used deliberately by a writer or character;

Unconscious irony: a statement or action which has significance for the reader of which the character is unaware;

Dramatic irony: when an action has an important significance that is obvious to the reader but not to one or more of the characters;

Tragic irony: when a character says (or does) something which will have a serious, even fatal, consequence for him/ her. The audience is aware of the error, but the character is not;

Verbal irony: the conscious use of particular words which are appropriate to what is being said.

Juxtaposition: literally putting two things side by side for purposes of comparison and/ or contrast.

Literal: the surface level of meaning that a statement has.

Melodramatic: action and/or dialogue that is inflated or extravagant – frequently used for comic effect.

Metaphor, metaphorical: the description of one thing by direct comparison with another (e.g. the coal-black night).

Extended metaphor: a comparison which is developed at length.

Mood: the feelings and emotions contained in and/ or produced by a work of art (text, painting, music, etc.).

Motif: a frequently repeated idea, image or situation in a text.

Motivation: why a character acts as he/she does – in modern literature motivation is seen as psychological.

Narrator: the voice that the reader hears in the text – not to be confused with the author.

Oxymoron: the juxtaposition of two terms normally thought of as opposite (e.g. the silent scream).

Paradox, paradoxical: a statement or situation which appears self-contradictory and therefore absurd.

Pathos: is pity, or rather the ability of a text to make the audience or reader feel pity.

Perspective: point of view from which a story, or an incident within a story, is told.

Catcher in the Rye by J.D. Salinger

Personified, personification: a simile or metaphor in which an inanimate object or abstract idea is described by comparison with a human.

Plot: a chain of events linked by cause and effect.

Protagonist: the character who initiates the action and is most likely to have the sympathy of the audience.

Realism: a text that describes the action in a way that appears to reflect life.

Rhetoric: any use of language designed to make the expression of ideas more effective (e.g. repetition, imagery, alliteration, etc.).

Sarcasm: stronger than irony – it involves a deliberate attack on a person or idea with the intention of mocking.

Setting: the environment in which the narrative (or part of the narrative) takes place.

Simile: a description of one thing by explicit comparison with another (e.g. my love is like a red, red rose).

Extended simile: a comparison which is developed at length.

Style: the way in which a writer chooses to express him/ herself. Style is a vital aspect of meaning since how something is expressed can crucially affect what is being written or spoken.

Suspense: the building of tension in the reader.

Symbol, symbolic, symbolism, symbolize: a physical object which comes to represent an abstract idea (e.g. the sun may symbolize life).

Themes: important concepts, beliefs and ideas explored and presented in a text.

Third person: third person singular is "he/ she/ it" and plural is "they" – authors often write novels in the third person.

Tone: literally the sound of a text – how words sound (either in the mouth of an actor or the head of a reader) can crucially affect meaning.

Tragic: King Richard III and Macbeth are both murderous tyrants, yet only Macbeth is a tragic figure. Why? Because Macbeth has the potential to be great, recognizes the error he has made and all that he has lost in making it, and dies bravely in a way that seems to accept the justice of the punishment. Richard III is, by contrast, simply and evil man, a villain.

A Study Guide

Literary terms activity

As you use each term in the study guide, fill in the definition of the term and include an example from the text to show how it is used. The first definition is supplied. Find an example in the text to complete it.

Term	Definition / Example
ambiguous, ambiguity	*when a statement is unclear in meaning – ambiguity may be deliberate or accidental.*
climax	
first person	
genre	
irony, ironic	

Catcher in the Rye by J.D. Salinger

Term	Definition
	Example
narrates, narrator	
narrative	
paradox, paradoxical	
pun	
symbol, symbolic, symbolism, symbolize	
voice	

A Study Guide

Term	Definition
	Example

Catcher in the Rye by J.D. Salinger

Graphic organizer

#1 Plot

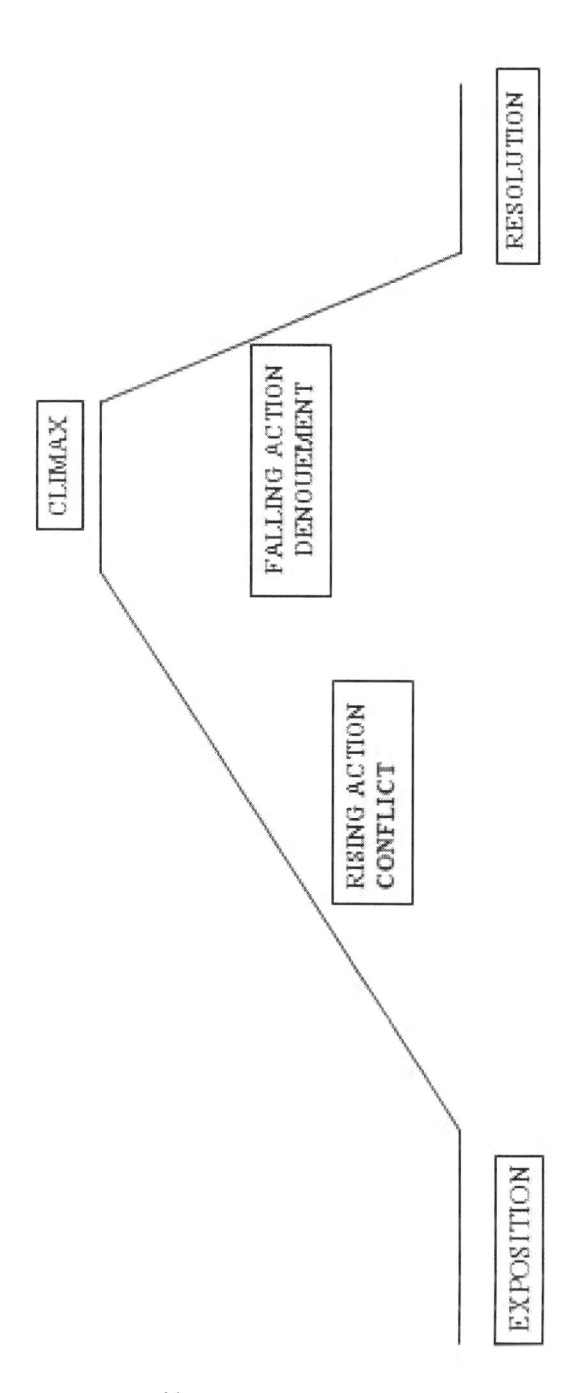

Plot graph for *Catcher in the Rye*

- EXPOSITION
- RISING ACTION / CONFLICT
- CLIMAX
- FALLING ACTION / DENOUEMENT
- RESOLUTION

#2 Different perspectives

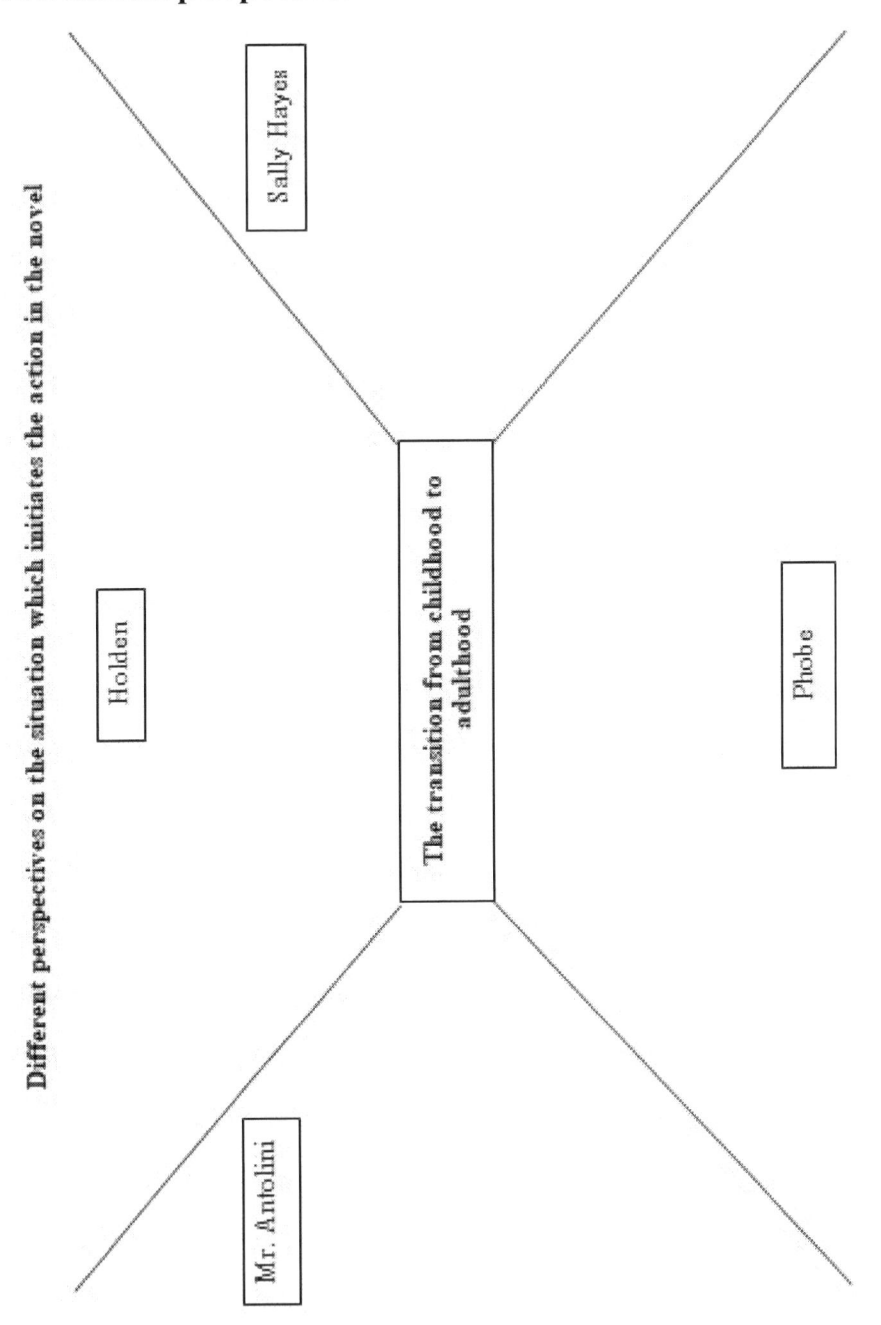

Different perspectives on the situation which initiates the action in the novel

- Sally Hayes
- Holden
- Mr. Antolini
- Phobe

Center: The transition from childhood to adulthood

Catcher in the Rye by J.D. Salinger
Revisiting A Controversial Text

Catcher in the Rye although originally published for adults, has become very popular with adolescent readers. It was included in *Time* magazine's 2005 list of 100 best English language novels written since 1923 and in 2003 was listed #15 on the BBC's survey "The Big Read". However, in 1961 and 1962 it was the most censored book in the USA. In the 1990s it appeared at #10 in the list of the most challenged books according to the American Library Association.

You should read Alexie Sherman's article, "Why the Best Kids Books Are Written in Blood" (*The Wall Street Journal*, June 9, 2011). It is easy to find on the Internet. Alexie Sherman is the author of the much-banned novel *The Absolutely True Diary of a Pert-Time Indian*. Here is perhaps his most powerful statement:

"Almost every day, my mailbox is filled with handwritten letters from students - teens and pre-teens - who have read my YA book and loved it. I have yet to receive a letter from a child somehow debilitated by the domestic violence, drug abuse, racism, poverty, sexuality, and murder contained in my book."
There is plenty of material here for discussion.

1. Which of these views most closely reflects your own?
a. Every parent must approve of a book before it is placed on a school reading list.
b. Every parent must approve of a book before it is required reading.
c. Every parent must approve of a book before it is taught in class.
d. Parents of individual students may opt out of reading any prescribed book; an acceptable
alternative will be provided.
e. Schools should be sensitive to parental views but ultimately schools set required reading.
f. A book should only be dropped if a majority of parents object to it.
If I have not even come close to stating your own view, formulate it yourself. Now argue it out in groups.

2. In groups, make a list of your ten favorite books - books that you think *every* young person should read.
Now work out how many of them would get through a. above.
Just to help you out, here are some really popular books that parents often seek to get banned: *Macbeth, Huck Finn, Tom Sawyer, Animal Farm, Catch-22, Beloved, The Grapes of Wrath,* and *Of Mice and Men*.
Were any of these on your group top-ten?

3. Research your own favorite book. Has it ever been banned anywhere? Has any individual or group ever tried to get it banned? Why?

A Study Guide

4. Of course, we all support the First Amendment, and we obviously want parents to be actively involved in their children's schools, but what do we do when parents want to ban books? How much say, if any, should the kids who are going to read the book have?

5. Write a letter either advocating or objecting to the banning of *Catcher* in schools. You need to be quite specific about your objections to / defense of the novel including examples and quotations. There is only one tiny catch: you have to take the side in this debate which is the *opposite* of what you actually believe.

6. As an alternative to #5, hold a mock School Board meeting in your classroom. With a vote at the end!

Catcher in the Rye by J.D. Salinger
Classroom Use of the Study Guide Questions

Although there are both closed and open questions in the Study Guide, very few of them have simple, right or wrong answers. They are designed to encourage in-depth discussion, disagreement, and (eventually) consensus. Above all, they aim to encourage students to go to the text to support their conclusions and interpretations.

I am not so arrogant as to presume to tell teachers how they should use this resource. I used it in the following ways, each of which ensured that students were well prepared for class discussion and presentations.

1. Set a reading assignment for the class and tell everyone to be aware that the questions will be the focus of whole class discussion the next class.

2. Set a reading assignment for the class and allocate particular questions to sections of the class (e.g. if there are four questions, divide the class into four sections, etc.).

In class, form discussion groups containing one person who has prepared each question and allow time for feedback within the groups.

Have feedback to the whole class on each question by picking a group at random to present their answers and to follow up with class discussion.

3. Set a reading assignment for the class, but do not allocate questions.

In class, divide students into groups and allocate to each group one of the questions related to the reading assignment the answer to which they will have to present formally to the class.

Allow time for discussion and preparation.

4. Set a reading assignment for the class, but do not allocate questions.

In class, divide students into groups and allocate to each group one of the questions related to the reading assignment.

Allow time for discussion and preparation.

Now reconfigure the groups so that each group contains at least one person who has prepared each question and allow time for feedback within the groups.

5. Before starting to read the text, allocate specific questions to individuals or pairs. (It is best not to allocate all questions to allow for other approaches and variety. One in three questions or one in four seems about right.) Tell students that they will be leading the class discussion on their question. They will need to start with a brief presentation of the issues and then conduct a question and answer session. After this, they will be expected to present a brief review of the discussion.

6. Having finished the text, arrange the class into groups of 3, 4 or 5. Tell each group to select as many questions from the Study Guide as there are members of the group.

A Study Guide

Each individual is responsible for drafting out a written answer to one question, and each answer should be a substantial paragraph.

Each group as a whole is then responsible for discussing, editing and suggesting improvements to each answer, which is revised by the original writer and brought back to the group for a final proof reading followed by revision.

This seems to work best when the group knows that at least some of the points for the activity will be based on the quality of all of the answers.

Catcher in the Rye by J.D. Salinger

To the Reader

Ray strives to make his texts the best that they can be. If you have any comments or question about this book *please* contact the author through his email: **villageswriter@gmail.com**

Visit his website **http://www.raymooreauthor.com**

Also by Ray Moore:

Books are available from amazon.com as paperbacks and some from online eBook retailers.

Fiction:

The Lyle Thorne Mysteries: each book features five tales from the Golden Age of Detection:

Investigations of The Reverend Lyle Thorne
Further Investigations of The Reverend Lyle Thorne
Early Investigations of Lyle Thorne
Sanditon Investigations of The Reverend Lyle Thorne
Final Investigations of The Reverend Lyle Thorne
Lost Investigations of The Reverend Lyle Thorne
Official Investigations of Lyle Thorne
Clerical Investigations of The Reverend Lyle Thorne

Non-fiction:

The ***Critical Introduction series*** is written for high school teachers and students and for college undergraduates. Each volume gives an in-depth analysis of a key text:

"The Stranger" by Albert Camus: A Critical Introduction (Revised Second Edition)
"The General Prologue" by Geoffrey Chaucer: A Critical Introduction
"Pride and Prejudice" by Jane Austen: A Critical Introduction
"The Great Gatsby" by F. Scott Fitzgerald: A Critical Introduction

The Text and Critical Introduction series differs from the Critical introduction series as these books contain the original text and in the case of the medieval texts an interlinear translation to aid the understanding of the text. The commentary allows the reader to develop a deeper understanding of the text and themes within the text.

"Sir Gawain and the Green Knight": Text and Critical Introduction
"The General Prologue" by Geoffrey Chaucer: Text and Critical Introduction
"The Wife of Bath's Prologue and Tale" by Geoffrey Chaucer: Text and Critical Introduction
"Heart of Darkness" by Joseph Conrad: Text and Critical Introduction

A Study Guide

"The Sign of Four" by Sir Arthur Conan Doyle Text and Critical Introduction
"A Room with a View" By E.M. Forster: Text and Critical Introduction
"Oedipus Rex" by Sophocles: Text and Critical Introduction
"Henry V" by William Shakespeare: Text and Critical Introduction
Jane Austen: The Complete Juvenilia: Text and Critical Introduction

Study Guides - listed alphabetically by author

Study Guides offer an in-depth look at aspects of a text. They generally include an introduction to the characters, genre, themes, setting, tone of a text. They also may include activities on helpful literary terms as well as graphic organizers to aid understanding of the plot and different perspectives of characters.

* denotes also available as an eBook
"ME and EARL and the Dying GIRL" by Jesse Andrews: A Study Guide
Study Guide to "Alias Grace" by Margaret Atwood*
Study Guide to "The Handmaid's Tale" by Margaret Atwood*
"Pride and Prejudice" by Jane Austen: A Study Guide
"Moloka'i" by Alan Brennert: A Study Guide
"Wuthering Heights" by Emily Brontë: A Study Guide *
Study Guide on "Jane Eyre" by Charlotte Brontë*
"The Myth of Sisyphus" by Albert Camus: A Study Guide
"The Stranger" by Albert Camus: A Study Guide
"The Myth of Sisyphus" and "The Stranger" by Albert Camus: Two Study Guides *
Study Guide to "Death Comes to the Archbishop" by Willa Cather
"The Awakening" by Kate Chopin: A Study Guide
Study Guide to Seven Short Stories by Kate Chopin
Study Guide to "Ready Player One" by Ernest Cline
Study Guide to "Disgrace" by J. M. Coetzee
"The Meursault Investigation" by Kamel Daoud: A Study Guide
Study Guide on "Great Expectations" by Charles Dickens*
"The Sign of Four" by Sir Arthur Conan Doyle: A Study Guide *
Study Guide to "Manhattan Beach" by Jennifer Egan
"The Wasteland, Prufrock and Poems" by T.S. Eliot: A Study Guide
Study Guide on "Birdsong" by Sebastian Faulks*
"The Great Gatsby" by F. Scott Fitzgerald: A Study Guide
"A Room with a View" by E. M. Forster: A Study Guide
"Looking for Alaska" by John Green: A Study Guide
"Paper Towns" by John Green: A Study Guide
Study Guide to "Turtles All the Way Down" by John Green
Study Guide to "Florida" by Lauren Groff
Study Guide on "Catch-22" by Joseph Heller *
"Unbroken" by Laura Hillenbrand: A Study Guide

Catcher in the Rye by J.D. Salinger
"The Kite Runner" by Khaled Hosseini: A Study Guide
"A Thousand Splendid Suns" by Khaled Hosseini: A Study Guide
"The Secret Life of Bees" by Sue Monk Kidd: A Study Guide
Study Guide on "The Invention of Wings" by Sue Monk Kidd
Study Guide to "Fear and Trembling" by Søren Kierkegaard
"Go Set a Watchman" by Harper Lee: A Study Guide
Study Guide to "Pachinko" by Min Jin Lee
"On the Road" by Jack Keruoac: A Study Guide
Study Guide on "Life of Pi" by Yann Martel*
Study Guide to "Death of a Salesman" by Arthur Miller
Study Guide to "The Bluest Eye" by Toni Morrison
Study Guide to "Reading Lolita in Tehran" by Azir Nafisi
Study Guide to "The Sympathizer" by Viet Thanh Nguyen
"Animal Farm" by George Orwell: A Study Guide
Study Guide on "Nineteen Eighty-Four" by George Orwell
Study Guide to "The Essex Serpent" by Sarah Perry
Study Guide to "Selected Poems" and Additional Poems by Sylvia Plath*
"An Inspector Calls" by J.B. Priestley: A Study Guide
Study Guide to "Cross Creek" by Marjorie Kinnan Rawlings
"Esperanza Rising" by Pam Munoz Ryan: A Study Guide
Study Guide to "The Catcher in the Rye" by J.D. Salinger
"Where'd You Go, Bernadette" by Maria Semple: A Study Guide
"Henry V" by William Shakespeare: A Study Guide
Study Guide on "Macbeth" by William Shakespeare *
"Othello" by William Shakespeare: A Study Guide *
Study Guide on "Antigone" by Sophocles*
"Oedipus Rex" by Sophocles: A Study Guide
"Cannery Row" by John Steinbeck: A Study Guide
"East of Eden" by John Steinbeck: A Study Guide
"The Grapes of Wrath" by John Steinbeck: A Study Guide
"Of Mice and Men" by John Steinbeck: A Study Guide*
"The Goldfinch" by Donna Tartt: A Study Guide
Study Guide to "The Hate U Give" by Angie Thomas
"Walden; or, Life in the Woods" by Henry David Thoreau: A Study Guide
Study Guide to "Cat's Cradle" by Kurt Vonnegut
"The Bridge of San Luis Rey" by Thornton Wilder: A Study Guide *
Study Guide on "The Book Thief" by Markus Zusak

Study Guides available only as e-books:
Study Guide on "Cross Creek" by Marjorie Kinnan Rawlings.
Study Guide on "Heart of Darkness" by Joseph Conrad:
Study Guide on "The Mill on the Floss" by George Eliot
Study Guide on "Lord of the Flies" by William Golding

A Study Guide

Study Guide on "Nineteen Eighty-Four" by George Orwell
Study Guide on "Henry IV Part 2" by William Shakespeare
Study Guide on "Julius Caesar" by William Shakespeare
Study Guide on "The Pearl" by John Steinbeck
Study Guide on "Slaughterhouse-Five" by Kurt Vonnegut

Readers' Guides

Readers' Guides offer an introduction to important aspects of the text and questions for personal reflection and/or discussion. Guides are written for individual readers who wish to explore texts in depth and for members of Reading Circles who wish to make their discussions of texts more productive.

A Reader's Guide to Becoming by Michelle Obama
A Reader's Guide to Educated: A Memoir by Tara Westover

New titles are added regularly.

Teacher resources:

Ray also publishes many more study guides and other resources for classroom use on the 'Teachers Pay Teachers' website:

http://www.teacherspayteachers.com/Store/Raymond-Moore

Made in the USA
Lexington, KY
04 June 2019